CW00467947

Printed i

www

Supporte
and Wild Duck Productions

www.isidore.uk

All further information at:
www.leere.co.uk
www.facebook.com/leerecollective

Front Cover: *'Image of Magic Bus' by Jolly Good Print*

Front Inside Cover: *'Manchester City Guide'*
by Gary Venn via www.escapeintolife.com

Back Inside Cover: *'The Storm on the Sea of Galilee'*
by Rembrandt van Rijn via www.filcatholic.org

Back Cover: *'Bee in the City Photograph' by Simon Monaghan*

Visit: www.visitmanchester.com
www.whitworth.manchester.ac.uk

Foreword

(by Nem Tomlinson, L'Arche Manchester)

L'Arche is a world-wide movement started nearly 60 years ago in France. There are now almost 160 Communities across 38 countries where people with and without learning disabilities share life together.

Started initially to meet the needs of those with disabilities who had been placed in larger institutions, often from childhood, it quickly became apparent that in living alongside one another something quite beautiful and revolutionary was happening. Conventional roles like 'carer' and 'cared for' were quickly broken down and instead our shared humanity and our need of each other became evident.

The huge, old institutions no longer exist in the UK but systemic oppression of people with learning disabilities has continued. Institutional abuse such as that discovered at Winterbourne View has continued. DNR orders placed on the files of people with learning disabilities without consultation or permission during the Covid-19 pandemic highlight a lack of regard for the value of such individuals. And there continue to be examples of people with learning disabilities stuck in long stay hospitals without clear ways out.

L'Arche is not perfect. We have our own lessons to learn and oversights to examine. At the same time, we are attempting to be a sign that the world can be different. Across our Communities, we celebrate the gifts of people with learning disabilities and build mutual relationships between all Community members where transformation can take place. L'Arche, for many of us, has been a school in being human and a place to imagine a different way of being.

The people with learning disabilities have been our greatest teachers. Much of this is through being primed for joy; a readiness to see moments of beauty and blessing in unexpected places. A shared joke over a meal, a dance party over the washing up, the everyday story signed over a cup of tea. A different pace; a different way of seeing the world.

I hope you'll get some sense of this captured in a joint adventure on a bus travelling down the Oxford and Wilmslow Road Corridor.

Nem Tomlinson (L'Arche Manchester)
www.larchemanchester.org.uk

In memory of
Andrea Shaw

Rumi, Number and Gridlock
(in Chorlton-on-Medlock)

by leere

'All journeys have secret destinations of which the traveller is unaware.'
- Martin Buber

From Bluebell House to Platt Fields Park

The buses …
The 140's …
The business of numbers …
There are enough of them
Sailing down Oxford Road
A flotilla
Sometimes in clusters
Of up to six or seven
In the measurable rain
Between 50%
And 57 %
Precipitation
Needs total concentration
Heading
For the 140's
'A major bus corridor'
Declares Wikipedia
Something grander
For Andrea and I
Sporting sailor hats
Sailor suits
Coats and warm vests
Suitably dressed
Since around
7.51
At our harbour hideout
Where we would map
Our nautical route
Ready to tackle
The seemingly
Forgotten

Location
Dubbed
The 'Chorlton-on-Medlock' section
Of that 'major bus corridor'
With its own rich
Unlikely assortment
Of persona
Of wonder
Of aroma
Of number
All leaping out at you
Must
Then
Keep alert
Like a couple of feline travellers
Pausing before every sign
Each approach
To scrutinise
The rule of number
The mystical
Patterns
Of the worldwide Ummah
Peaking out
Through the M14 zone
The B5117
Adjoining the A6010
… for a brief segment …
A four pound 80 Day Rider
As it was
Back then
Numerous bus providers
Along that linear route
You can catch a fleeting glimpse

Of its stretch

In the city

From the tracks

At the perimeter

Of the cramped platforms

On Oxford Road

Railway

Station

But in stark

Bus, boat and navigational parlance

Our landing stage

Was up by the iron railings

Opposite the high rise

At Platt Fields

Park

Good as any place to embark

Technically Wilmslow Road

So I'm told

Destination set

A digit away in postcode

Usually around 10.07

Voyage named 'Bluebell Jaunt'

We would amble

Up the Lane

Via the ginnel

Like swaying mannequins

Gauging wind direction

Flowers poking through

Children's playground noise

Filtering in

And out

Of the damp air

As water levels rose

And puddles
Splattered our toes
Shoes fastened tightly
At about 7.39
And soon into sight
Comes the hazy quayside post
The boundary
To 'the People's Park'
Of South Manchester
That's where we tended
To wait
Most mornings
Rain swept
Accepting the unruly
Bus arrival times
Eager to start out
On our aquatic manoeuvres
Like two delicate pond skaters
Tiny
In the oceans of the city
And I would wonder
What might the puckish day
Throw up
For one feels
Most like
One is at sea
Balancing oneself
And another
From the splashes of disharmony
Grappling with urgency
Uncertainty
Swinging
Rocking

Rolling
Squinting
Amid the patterns of rain
The business of numbers …
On the 140's …
The buses …

Over 700
Unemployed men
Engaged
In the configuration
Of the public parkland
At Platt Hall Estate
The trees, the diagonal paths
Delicate shrubs
The construction of the lake
And the island
Art and movement
A grassy unity
Being spun
Outwards
Upwards
Progressive designs
Insider drafts
Sketches
Plans
Once anticipated
For this 'green lung of the city'
By Architect William Royle
Of Rusholme
And
Outsiders
Finding a way back in

700 of them
A hive of innovation
The Park as sanctuary
Formally opened in 1910
A different noise back then
And today
Here ...bound in time
Andrea
And Teddy
And I
Dressed in the nautical costumes of our day
In our inward silence
Before the seas

From Platt Fields Park to Steve Biko Building

The buses …
The 140's …
The business of numbers …
Negotiating the broken pavement
The single step up
Onto the vessel
Immediately less exposed
Drying out
And once afloat
Drifting from the marina platform
There would be the usual
Quick driver dialogue
Bus pass presentation
Bus conventions
Hesitation
And we'd shuffle
Along the lower deck
Preparing to stand
To bend
And to squeeze
To apologise
And to utter
'Please can I ..?'
Some light cajoling
Tailored whispers punctuated with aggrieved sighs
As people freeze
To maximise room
Andrea and I
Eventually
Finding the seats
We were chasing
Prioritize
A deep breath
And to breathe …
A little easier
I strive to fix Andrea's damp hair

Give her hand a gentle reassuring tap
Watch her soft and temperate eyes
Comb the space
Then check correct ticket
Safety of wallet
Phone
Keys
In the right pocket
Or was it the left ?
Glasses beginning to steam up
Mine !
Seafaring smiles
What's a little steam
On a bus boat like this ..?
As long as we can detect
Roughly where we are heading
And be entirely ready
To repeat
The whole drill once more
Preparing to stand
To bend
And to squeeze
To apologise
And to utter
'Please can I ..?'
Some light cajoling
Awaiting tailored whispers
Interspersed with aggrieved sighs
As people freeze
To maximise room
We shuffle along
The lower deck
Double check
So as to hopefully
Disembark
Somewhere near Whitworth Park
As a pair

A right pair
Among
The business of numbers …
On the 140's …
The buses …

55,000
Bit of a jump in number !
Approximately 55,000 items
In its extensive collection
At the Whitworth Art Gallery
Opened in 1908
With the guiding hand
The help
Of Robert Darbishire
Local philanthropist
Health clinic now duly named after him
Tucked up on Walmer Street
Well Being and Art
Treating and healing
Across communities
Soothingly
Silently
Discreetly

55,000
An impressive gallery
Anyone been counting ?
Counting street signs
Museum pieces
Counting the hours
In bus and shipping lanes
Counting numbers ?

My concern
Just now
Is

For
One
Four pound 80 Day Rider
And one Greater Manchester travel pass
Safe
In case
Of any possible
Later
Official
Stagecoach
Inspection

The buses …
The 140's …
The business of numbers …
Strong grip on Andrea's sleeve
Just about to partake
In a little
Quick driver dialogue
For the second time
Negotiate the step down
By the multiple bus shelters
Brimming with sea sorts
Bus hoppers
Shoppers
More students
Fella jumps out
Bus breaks
Shrieks and yelps along the decks
Luggage rack rumble
Lots of stumbling
And mumbling
As people try
Finding their feet again
Chap shouts
In the road
At another driver

On one of the many
140's
Something about being
Eligible
For a concessionary fare
Unfairness laid bare
Waves a permit of sorts
Like a holy manuscript
Roars about his age
And all that
Then dissolves
Somewhere
Near the Poundland store
One soul begins
To pick up
Scattered coins from the grubby floor
Of the bus
… I mean 'the boat' …
Another
Woman
Of African descent
Gathers her shopping
Pulls it close
Food for the week
A child's toy doll is safely returned
To its owner
Food for the weak
Broken conversation
Resuming
And we're afloat again
Possible later connections
Academic routes and directions
Maths exam questions
Numerical advantages
In football league tables
Rashford's contribution
Across the nation

Talking red, white and blue
Statistics
Mystifying comprehension
Altruistic figures
Capturing our attention
Not quitting
In the face of numbers
The business of numbers …
On the 140's …
The buses …

In excess of
9.5 million
… an ever increasing number …
Of meals for children
And for families
Provided
Since
3
2020
Throughout the present crisis
Marcus and FareShare
Doing their
Authentic
Compassionate thing
For our hungry young things
In postcodes
Juxtaposed
Worlds away
From the ubiquitous TV food shows
Hardly credible
In a G7 country
Number 10
Calling out
Number 10
A striker's goal
A tender tale

Limitless
Measureless
<u>*United*</u>
Human
Effort

The buses …
The 140's …
The business of numbers …
Okay
So
We've missed our stop
Now
At the flagship Students' Union
The 'Steve Biko Building'
Pavements alive
Bursting with ideas
Of the age
Beyond the age
Leaflet and pamphlet
Being handed over
Like 'Merry Christmases'
Another addition
To the pilgrim's pocket
Youth
Energy
Unquestionably
Out
And about
Seizing the day
Dipping deep into news streams
The array
Of contesting narrative
Around the direction of the planet
We all inhabit
Weather carefree
Making contact

On this damp morn
In street force
Near drama halls
They press
Literature and prose
Into palms
All small cogs of change
As the Oxford Road traffic
Crawls
Pours
Towards the conurbation
These young hearts
Beating for change
Signs of the struggle
Still booming
Biko
Resonant
Round this region
The call to 'Come Spirit'
Pitches high here
We sure-fire live in our hopes
… don't we ?
We habitual mystics
Of scrawled city and desert prayer
Living in possibilities shared
Born of belief
In something better
So clear the way
Of congestion and obstruction
Hold number to a minimum
Decipher and decode
In the road if you have to …
We can get real hung up
On numbers
Data drenched
Easily miss the moment
Outside of the dictates and commands of the clock

You can get a mighty shock
By looking up a few names
And ages
In the Torah
Or in the pages
Of longevity myths
Persian fables
The supercentenarians
Noah's doing well
In the floods of time
Reached
The tender age of 950 years
Spotted in Manchester
Braving the weather
Using his bus pass
On the 140's …
Oblivious to number
Women and men
Prophetess
And priest
Waking folk from their urban slumber
Youthful in witness
To everything
East and West
Beyond our comprehension
Calculation
Concentration
Crossing the busy artery
Now
With Andrea
Hold on
Andrea holds on
I clutch at 'sacred space'
And I think I've spotted it
Holy Name
A bit of Jesuit solace
The Alpha and the Omega

Someplace
Amidst the motion
The endeavour
We seek an oceanic scope
Sincere reach
Whilst chipping away
At justice
Daily
Remembering
6
9
77
Port Elizabeth
Amid
The business of numbers …
On the 140's …
The buses …

Close to 100,000 people studying
At the five Higher Education Institutions
Across these ten boroughs
18, 000 international students
The University of Manchester Students' Union
The UK's largest
No need to make a note of the figures
We're not in the business of losers
Or of winners
Or for that matter
… Numbers

From Steve Biko Building to Coffee Shop Questions

The buses …
The 140's …
The business of numbers …
Finally
We're back on terra firma
Having done our heavenly thing
Needing some refreshment
After such maritime and roadside excitement
We would hunt down
An appropriate venue
One serving cookies
Maybe caramel slices
Chocolate brownies
'Cakies'… says Andrea
Treats easily balanced
Then scour the space to find our seats
And from that one station by the window
Watch the precious drift of the day
Gauge the tolerance and position
The mission and disposition of others
Through our café encounters
Explore
The shapes and sizes of confectionary
Of cups and saucers
And customers
Gazing aimlessly
Flying through word and digit
On handheld screens
Engrossed
In phone patterns
Unconditional
Configurations
'These are the shapes and the fashions of the world'
They would say
'How dull'

We would say
'These are the shapes and the fashions of our world
… try them for size !'
Café encounters
Cafe reflections
Lasting roughly fifty minutes
Away
From
The business of numbers …
The 140's …
The buses …

Now for my confession

You should never
Ask a woman
Her age

Andrea is nineteen
By her own estimation
Youthful as Hebe
Before the swirling elements
At the seat of Olympus
In truth
I never actually knew
Andrea's real age
The flat figure
We lodge in mind
Inscribe on the mental page
Life was too eventful
Too full
Of the present mysteries
Concealed
Then revealed
At these common intervals
During sea frolics
And those trifles

Incidentals
Around age
Ages
Remained inconsequential
She loved her biscuits
Her 'Cakies'
'Milky Ways'
And 'sweeties'
That fact
Was not so confidential
Among our close knit Team
Indeed
It must be factored in
To any time spent together
Coffee and snack consumed
I might be in a rush to leave
Bus in mind
No timetable required
In this bubble of motion and commotion
Negotiating
Those swinging glass exits
Of the coffee shop
Delicately
By rotating steadily with one's hips
Hand in hand
With your friend
With Andrea
Glad
In our rather unorthodox exit
That Mary
Was ever ready
To help with the heavy door
Back onto the busiest street
European semblances
New spheres of learning
Illuminated entrances
Is that the sun we spot ..?

Right here
Among student
Preacher
Lecturer
Types
Shining bright
On Musos
Goths
'Weirdos'
Hoboes
Relishing difference
Playing at hopeful
Midst the homeless faces
Those with some foreign status
The artist exiled
The poet reconciled
And traces
On each one of them
Of the last downpour
About the base of their bags
Their coats and hats
Shiny sailor suits
Held in their arms
So as to dry out speedily
In the aforementioned sun
Just briefly
Serenely
Holding to
Mancunian mystery
As if in dance or trance
Hacienda trickery
There
I'd be humming
The Roses
And Andrea would shout
'Stop singing'
Arm in arm

Probing opinion
Strolling
Looking out
For the next one
Shuffling along
That 'major bus corridor'
Back
In the business of numbers …
Of the 140's …
The buses …

Ford Madox Brown
1821 to 1893
Depicting work
Time
And interaction
Victorian scenes
One of his most famous images
'The Last of England'
Painted between 1852 and 1855
Two empty faces
Sheltering
Aboard a boat
Perhaps a Stage Coach ?
Hands clasped in deep unknowing
Incredulous
A future cast overboard
Sold in March 1859
For 325 Guineas

The wanted and the unwanted
What we keep
And what we disregard
What we come to know
And what we dare to start
Together

Coffee Shop Questions
Number 1: WHO'S UP FOR A SEA CHANGE?

Did you catch
'The Cloud Gardener'
During the pandemic months ?
Nurturing away
In fidelity
On Nature
Art at its very best
High above the city
Setting the work of the sky
Against the stresses of the sea
Sitting comfortable …
Amid dove
And olive branch
Vigilantly

Or

Mayor
Burnham
Before the pandemic months ?
Measuring
Air pollution levels
Carbon emissions
Stating his position
On Clean Air Zones
Our future prospects
In serious tones
Spelling out alternatives
To the pressing traffic
No minor matter
Vehicles lumbering
In manic number
On this stretch
Of the B5117

Nitrogen dioxide levels
Causing more than 1200 premature deaths
Every year
Across
The 10 metropolitan boroughs
Of Greater Manchester
Needlessly

Or

Do you detect
The roaring beast
Still ravenous
After the pandemic months ?
The rumble of a thundering avarice
That can only be tamed by defiance
Non-compliance
In the best of this city tradition
The smell of honest protest
Any means of keeping young hearts afloat
Aware they beat so rapidly for change
Like a steady drum
Before a chorus of transformation
The latest insurrection bubbles
As Youth picks up on what still troubles
A Northern populace
Echoes of Peterloo
16
8
1819
Defy
Scepticism
Around 'Me Too'
Climate Indifference
The sound of
Drum
Pride

The fire inside
Solidarity
Empathy
Over cries of
'Dispersal by the military'
Remembering Agecroft
Severe and repeated winters of division
Pits once 'sunk'
Communities sure to follow
Indifferent rulings
Made in clandestine corridors
Not so different
Throughout
The ages
Age

A pitched resistance
Attracting the bee
Net zero the key
Taking the knee
Safe havens
For the weary refugee
Here and now
Any sea change
Needs its pioneers
To take hope of course
And push it forth
So it bursts through the depths
Of complacency
They seem to spring from this habitat
Like captains setting out against the wind
With brighter coloured sails
Taking
Smarter routes
Shifting gears
Tacking
Manchester style

… like Simply Cycling
Out at Wythenshawe
The Cladiators
Demanding safer homes
In domestic law
The Hitman
Jabbing with Barnabus
The Cloud Gardener
Mayor Burnham
Mr Martin Hibbert
19
Thousand feet up
From sea level
In his wheelchair …
Our Kids
Taking hope of course
And pushing it forth
So it bursts through the walls
Unashamedly
Courageously
Intentionally
A New Order ?

Coffee Shop Questions
Number 2 : WHAT WILL CARRY US THROUGH STORMS?

How swift
The spirals and sorrows of the dark
Can gather
On horizons
Clouds of a wearing
A tearing
Guilt
Becoming weighty
Forms of a previous life
Peer through
As villains revisiting each intrusive scene
The forced adjustments
Adaptations
To loss
The reality
The cost
Of hearing the words
'Never again …'
Spoken about a friend

Sick with worry
Struggling to hold on
To flailing timber
Metal
Glass
Or petal
Any object within the vessel
Turmoil
Breeding turmoil
Like watching walls crumble
Crash on inner floors of jewels
… be it
By trial
By denial

In phases
Intentions
Missing the mark
Transgressions
Casting us overboard
In whatever city or region
You can feel
Suddenly
That your soul is riding
Rolling
Undulating
Gasping
In Rembrant's 'Storm on the Sea
Of Gallilee'
The lost painting

In the mirrors of our plagued existence
We are there
Unrecognizable

Then

Hear me out

When the enervative picture is beheld within
Absorbed all it can
When Man attacks himself in private
In public
In tears
In fear
With the rods
Of strife and blame
Mistrust and shame
Confronted now by his waywardness
There seems little hope of return
To waters clear
To the 360 degree

Twist
And shout
Of Teshuvah
Of redirecting the vessel
Of seizing the ship's helm

Dry your eyes from the sting
And salt of the sea
To look again into the eye of 'The Storm'
To the lost painting
For alternative realms
Are all about us
Silently
The faces in the boat
13
A cursed number
Adopt a more distinct feminine dimension
Women of voice and of no voice
Purpose and trajectory
Singing mercy
Steer us back
Amid this arena
To eye again countless traces of presence
Clear along the shoreline
The winter and summer hills leap into view
The tender seasons greet
Reacquainted with Creation
And our small part in it
Women of voice and of no voice
Pull us away from the tempest
Christ never absent
Dragging to shore
Those who enter the calm

Of their
Calling
Those
Who can place
The Day
Drawing
On the lost art of Being
Those
Like Andrea Shaw
Jackanory Jill
Mo
The Seven Sisters
Pearl Marguerite …
The Pankhursts holding the mast
A crew
Complete
In the 'steadfast' belief
Of the Psalmist
An acute wisdom
Where seeds of the flower are diffused again
Direction restored
Compassion
Now filling the Baroque scene
13
Plus Christ never absent
And
Man
Then feels the wind and the rain subside
Tides calm
Pale and steady waves return
He sees the journey clear
The treasury
Of a sober destination …
So look at any storm
Like I now look at 'The Storm on the Sea
Of Galilee'
The lost painting

Coffee Shop Questions
Number 3: WHERE TO CAST ANCHOR DEAR SAILORS?

Be it art
Rediscovered
Or be it the push of hearts
Beating for change
In shaping
A sustained
Calling
Place
The Day
Take stock
For the protracted grip of 'the Self'
Can swell up
And the echo of an old song can sweep in
A childish song I guess
Easily reworked into verse
Nonetheless …

'We say the city can kill you
For it's got its own rules
As to what you do …

We say the city can kill you
For it's got its own rules
As to what rings true …'

Wednesday afternoons
Arrived
And valiantly
As warriors
With presence and with prana
There was the invitation to leave
Number
The city
To enter

A Hive
Of Friendship
Interior silence
So to meet with the daughter of peace
Yoga
… Or maybe her sibling
Prayer …
Losing the bit that says
Keep human intensity
Intense
Our core members
Breathe and move
Core muscles
Uncoil and relax
Any haunting 'disorders' eased
And the Present
Cosies up again
Like earth's fragile floor to truth
The mat before her
The path of patience
Open to transformation
Open to every form
Attached to none
Ability shines
Disability chimes
To the orchestra of humankind
With this gracious exercise
On Wednesday afternoons
… And that is enough
For there, we become part
Of the one vast sky
The clouds but brief judgements
The hush repairing
Our divided souls
Noise retreating
And we wrap the qualities we each hold
Soft

In the embalmment
Of community
That recognises the path to healing
Is in fact
Revealing oneself
As vulnerable
A work in progress
A painting now lost
Now found
The smile of 'an Other'
Fanning your very spirit before the routine task
As the Prophet once declared
Loud and clear
'The most excellent jihad
Is the conquest of one's self'

Be it art
Rediscovered
Or be it the push of hearts
Deafening
Beating for change
In shaping
A sustained
Calling
Place
The Day
Take stock
Sit comfortable
Play vigilantly
Ever watchful for the dove
And the olive branch
Vigilant
On one's holistic health

So, how *might* we use our ticket and bus pass ?

The buses …
The 140's …
The business of numbers …
Once
On a balmy June afternoon
I recall
12.19 would see us
Sail past the Aquatics Centre
Alighting at the Principal Hotel
Travelling time free that day
Tea supped
Cups settling
On ceramic cradles
And echoing
Across the spacious
Art Deco designs
Wiping the table
Dabbing our mouths
Two visits to the loo
Bag skilfully packed
Andrea
Biding her time
Scrutinising
The professional classes
Gathering in their recreation
Every congregation and convention
Can inspire
Hints of summertime
Tapping at windows
Like excited children
Back outside around 13.22
Onto ground level
Urban birds
Bathing
In a gentle sunlight

Nearby
Behind street crevices
The call of 'Wonderwall'
Being belted out
From somewhere
Beneath the archways
Tall cranes on a building plot
Lights from the outdoor canopy
Of The Palace Theatre
Where Goodwin, Coogan and Dawson
Have all put a shift in
The whole notion
Of Manchester motion
Oxford 'Street' territory now …
I know !
End of the Road ?
River Medlock skirting city centre
A side door at the Palace
Wide open
Peeped in
Elvis impersonator
Calls out
'I was the One'
Across the traffic
The Palace intersection
Near the Station
She lived
She loved
She laughed,
I cried
Third time in a day
Before boarding
Again
The 140's
The buses
On that particular balmy June afternoon
I'm here recalling

13.48 by now
Spinning age
Spinning stages
Stretching the clocks before us
The business of numbers …
And of song …
On the 140's …
The buses …

The Palace Theatre
Capacity: 1955
Originally known as the 'Grand Old Lady'
Opened on 18th May 1891
At a cost of £40,500
Designed by Salford architect
Alfred Darbyshire
Took a direct hit
From a German bomb
During the Manchester Blitz
Of September 1940
Still standing
Just like 'The Grosvenor Picture Palace'
Little further up
Stage and widescreen
Tough as earth
Stubborn as rock
Around here
Where river weaves
Unnoticed
A city boundary line
To the seemingly
Forgotten
Location
Dubbed
'Chorlton-on-Medlock'

The 140's …
The buses …
The business of numbers …
When feeling especially bold
We might take ourselves
Over Canal Street
Up to St Peter's Square
For trams to outlying Altrincham
But that's getting into
Much stormier waters
Approaching Deansgate
Spinningfields
Another quarter
We've even been known to sample
The glitz and glamour
The dizzy stretches
Of 'MediaCityUK'
A stone's throw
From Salford's first Public Library
And the adventures of boys with guitars
But by then
We'd sort of lost interest
In the far and distant sea
Free woman
Free man
Forgetful that the rain had returned
Soon to be
Surrounded
By fellow wayfarers
More numbers than ever
Calmly
Doing their thing
About the metropolis
We knew within
We must return
Soon enough
To fixed measures of time

And place
If only
You could capture it
Bus buddies
Ship mates
Tram pals
A frame in that dry gallery space
A selfie could never do it justice
Andrea and I
Might even
Do the unthinkable
Stay on
Some 140 ..!
Venture entirely the other way
Southwards
Beyond the Oxford Road
Wilmslow Road
A5145
Way out of our depth now
Past
Owens Park Campus
Fallowfield
Withington
A wave goodbye to St Paul's
And 'the evil we do not want to do'
A nod to The Christie
Good among the contradictory
Further afield
A Journeying into green
Openings
The neat arrangements of Fletcher Moss
Botanical Gardens
Sizable driveways
Fronting the more spacious homes
The promise of Cheshire
Residence
And then

Asserting our independence
Interdependence
Our own foolishness
Like naughty schoolkids
Shoot
Back the other way
Just because we could
For the thrill of it !
Towards the Rusholme traffic
Ploughing on
To hear the bus brake
To see people sway
And hear them curse
And to absorb their smiles
And watch people amass
In the later afternoon
Their commute home
The surge of human travel
We were adrift
Aware
Kind to any stranger
Any sailor
We might meet encounter by chance
Carrying
Suitcase
School bag
Instrument
With RNCM stamp
Daily woes
Holdall
Phone
In company
Alone
Time we scoffed at
Surely not meant to be spent
Solely on devices
Costing crazy prices

Dealing with some
Perceived
Information
'Crisis'
Waiting on the ping of notifications
Looking for the next 'entertainment sensation'
Whilst missing this one
Variety is the touch
The spoken word
The grin splashed across the faces
Shining vividly
Good things
Albeit contradictory
And the scent of spices
Resurfacing
Adored from a window seat
Are we not too old for this ..?
Andrea and I
This sort of simple enjoyment ?
All the options spring open
When your heart
Runs away with you
In imagination and celebration
Like Sergio's late goal
Every day seems to be the start of summer
As if fluorescent buses of joy
Are being launched
Into the tranquil sea
What we could fill
With the gift of a day
Light free
Two becoming
Inwardly
Silent again
In Harmony
With Teddy
Unconscious

To
The business of numbers …
On the 140's …
The buses …

As a kid
I recollect
Adding together
The five
Numbers
Across the top
Of my tiny bus ticket
To see if it made
A total
Of 21
If it did
That was good luck
Bestowed on us
By some higher power
Still do it where possible
Whole days …
Determined
By a solitary
Bus ticket !

Make way
For Johnny Roadhouse
Born 13 January 1921
British musician
Self-taught
Saxophone specialist
Instrumentalist wizard
Opening up
His Oxford Road store
'Johnny Roadhouse Music'
In 1955
Presented with a Lifetime Achievement Award

By the Lord Mayor of Manchester
In 2005
Fraternising with Manchester's finest …
Music
Accessible
Keeping the older
Younger
And the young
Buoyant

So, how *did* we use our ticket and bus pass ?

The buses …
The 140's …
The business of numbers …
14.30 precisely
Andrea enjoying the ride
Still seated
Holding the rail
Gently letting
The day
Flow with the sails
Of the bus
On course
Wind getting up a little now
Through the narrow
Slender windows
Of our common craft
Passing the stop
For
Number 84
Plymouth Grove
The Gaskells' front door
That social circle rapport
Plenty of local resident
And student chatter
The characteristic
Buzz
About the night before
Pub life
Work plans
Film nights
Academic routes and directions
Replayed
Essays
Dissertations
Delayed

Passengers
All most courteous
Pleased to say
With our Andrea
Needing that bit more space
Than others, I guess
Not always true
Of some PSV drivers
Who can assume
That their service users
Need the very briefest
Of harbour stops
Worried about any timetable delays
Distractions
Protractions
However
On a fair and a flowing day
Compass friendly
Raising the best things aloft
Like the first pink rambling roses
In the drizzle of early May
We would find
Our channel
Eventually
Into port
Recharged
Ready to share
Those tales of the waves
And the currents
The creatures
The vessels
The buses …
The 140's …
The business of numbers …

Heading back
Sometime after 14.41

That's when it happened

At a point
Somewhere
On 'The Curry Mile'
A joy to hear
Alongside Anand Fashions
Where Alexandria boasts a petite, magnificent library
Pushed every worry
Behind me
Took me
Into a deeper reality
Exposed
What the great
Sufi writers
Call
'The barriers within yourself'
Those that you have built
Against truth
Over the painful drag of time
The affliction of number
On the 140's
Together
On the priority seats
It happened
Just there …
Andrea spoke softly

'… I love you'

Our stop
Still seemed some distance away
Words fell on me
Traffic halted
Number lifted
'Masha'Allah'
I knew there

I knew then
That I really did
Have a priority seat
Observing Andrea's
Understanding
Of our fussy and flawed
World
In which
Manchester
Reaches out
Speaks to us
In art and movement
In Being
Across identity
City United
With determination
A civic feature
All creeds
Colours
Capabilities
Breathing free of terror
Marching on
Despite the weather
Remembering
Lives
Their worth
Their shine
The
Arena
Victims
Twenty two of them
With
Love
That machine called purpose
Surging through
Above all else

Numbers do
Just seem to hang around
Uninvited
Like arbitrary pointers
To a place called 'home'
They don't really get much of a look in now
God bless 'em
So
In short
That's when
The business of numbers
Started slipping my mind
In favour of
Fewer numbers
The fidelity of numbers
Friendship over figures
Those we travel with …
Arm in arm
Calmly
Daily
The pressure and stress of number
Slipping
The vast business of numbers
Sliding
Just there
On the 140's …
The buses …

LS Lowry
Factory Sensitive
Wynford Dewhurst
Manchester's Monet
Ford Madox Brown
Pre Raphaelite
Henry Liverseege
Realising disability
Brothers

Men of voice
And of no voice
Travelling
Without fear of fanning hostile reaction
Through unique form
One form to another
Outsiders
Perceiving beauty and proportion
Without detraction
Men of voice
And of no voice
Outsiders
Confirming
That Art beckons the possible
Carrying us through purposelessness
Silently and brazenly
Buried within an inner revolution
The broadest appreciation
Of fraternity
Tender is the touch
Behind every storm
If you but look close

From Platt Fields to Bluebell House

The buses …
The 140's …
The business of numbers …
A quieter bus mood descending
Our boating days ending
Andrea would loosen her grip on the rail
And take both of my hands
For a choreographed exit
My legs might give a tremble
A shout to the driver
'This one pleeease...'
Forgetting any idea of that quick driver dialogue
For now
The bus would edge towards the stop
The marina platform
There might be a jolt
Another
A high pitched goodbye
Voiced the length of the deck
A child's soft cry
An imposing ringtone
The swish of the doors opening
Like a rush of wind through flowers
Bluebells
Forget me nots
Forever signs
This time we're both off safely
At the correct spot
And together
We'd skate lightly
Even somewhat merrily
Along the surface
Sea oblivious
Pavement aware
Sun enthused

And gracefully
Return along the paths once more
To amble
Down the Lane
Via the ginnel
To our harbour hideout
Much later than we thought
From our timeless
Ageless trip
Our sea jaunt
City venture
Possibly something grander
… for I felt
That we had spanned the Universe …
The 'Milky Way'
Multipack
In my left side pocket
Or was it the right ?
I had bought up at Poundland
If I wasn't too mean

£1.40
The 140's
19
45's
33's
Row A
Seats: 24 and 25
Grand Tier Tickets
For The Palace Theatre
If you're feeling plucky
A for Andrea
The best seats in the house
The priority seats
On a Greater Manchester Mystery Tour
Through M13
Or is it M14 ?

Gauging the tempo of the worldwide Ummah
Guessing the origins of the abacus
The B5117
Adjoining the A6010
... for a brief segment ...
Oxford Road
A four pound 80 Day Rider
20p in change
Andrea's pass
Deposited back in its tin
Dates you travel with
22
5
2017
Ages you travel with
19
Enigma codes
B for secondary
Number light
Where anything's possible in human life
Necessary
Now
Back to the Turing Tap
The draw of the honey pot
Memory heavy
New Year goals
Epiphany zones
6
1
2021
A Crossroads
We faced together
Comes flooding back
Into my mind
Two sea mates
Resting again
But best let numbers

Do their thing
I mean
Just
Accompany
Everything
One step at a time
From now on
Mulling over this new world order
The business of numbers …
On the 140's …
The buses …

Scarcely believable
That a rogue President
Once
Led a mission of fabrication
Spewing out hate
Fiddling statistics
Distorting the person
Drowning in digits
Parodying 'the Other'
For political traction
A glib reaction
A malady of power
When challenges
Are so real
Palpable
Right now
For the 1 billion people
Worldwide
Who live with some form of disability
15% of the earth's population
Who need us
To go beyond
The congestion of numbers
Stereotypes
Perpetuated

On screens
They need us
To immerse
And to journey wider
Into the immensity
Of human traffic
Of what we don't know
Don't want to know
The sea of diversity
Disability
Culture and gender
Sit
Stand and sway
Be the solid rock among histories
Between
Complexion
Expression
Connection
Affirmed
And made
Humanity unafraid

The buses …
The 140's ….
The business of numbers …
There are enough of them
Sailing down Oxford Road
And we certainly
Sailed them
In our short time together
Rain sodden
Avoiding puddle
And spontaneous
Roadside pond
Yes
As a pair
A right pair

We would reappear
From our trip on the high seas
Always
In time for tea
Tables of communion focus
A brew
… 'another cup of tea'
That 'Milky Way'
Some night time TV
Strictly
Together
In the cosy living room
At Bluebell House
Fully integrated
Shared
Space
All abilities
Vulnerabilities
Working
At tranquillity
Infinite determination
Through
The business of numbers …
On the 140's …
The buses …

Andrea left this world

3
11
2020

And I can't begin …

I mean …

I couldn't tell you …

Even now

Here

Within this poetry laid bare

… I never actually knew

Andrea's exact age …

Does that then
Perhaps make
A life
Less
Rooted
Significant
Our connection
Of less value ..?
Numbers
Passed
Figures
Eroded
On our trips
Only smiles and presence
Persist
The simple glee
Behind our voyages
Across the city of the Bee
In landscape terms
I sing to myself now
'She's my waterfall'

Life
Today
For sure
Is less eventful

Than it was before
I no longer
Squint
Amid the patterns of rain
Pre-occupied
Merely
With the business of numbers
The 140's
The buses
But hold
To river
Beside the road
Its twists and its depths
The faces along
That stretch
Of 'Chorlton-on-Medlock'
In some soulful embrace
And so try to let numbers
Do their thing
I mean
Just
Accompany
Everything
And only be ready
To set sail again
Through any weather
Even if it means a soaking in the street of faith
Try as Rumi said
'Start a huge, foolish project
Like Noah …
For it makes absolutely
No difference
What people think of you'
So I
Sit comfortably …
Still
With Teddy

With Spirit
Vigilant
In the truth of our unawareness
In the youth of our limitations
Even
When
Gridlocked

AMDG

Acknowledgements

'Rumi, Number and Gridlock' is dedicated to the enthusiastic and hardworking team of core members, assistants and volunteers (… both past and present!) at 'L'Arche Manchester'. Their spirit of inclusivity and co-operation provided the inspiration behind this poem. We are most grateful to Nem Tomlinson (Community Leader) for her excellent foreword to the book and to David Ward for his early reading of the text.

Afzal Khan, MP for Manchester Gorton, gave much encouragement in the early phases of the book and this is warmly acknowledged. Thank you again to Erica Stones for all support and detailed advice in the process of compiling the 'city trilogy', and to Liza Monaghan for proof reading the series with speed and efficiency.

Tom Pearson at Isidore and Wild Duck Productions has offered thoughtful guidance and invaluable practical assistance during the course of the last 18 months. We are indebted to him. Thank you also to Mark Fenlon and the Team at Jolly Good Print for stepping in to ensure that this piece in the jigsaw was successfully completed. Please see the link below to order the earlier books in the trilogy.

Finally, by way of gratitude to Maureen Monaghan, thank you for all patience and insight, for mugs of tea and a sympathetic ear, particularly when various obstacles cropped up on route !

Discover more about the work of L'Arche' at:
www.larchemanchester.org.uk

Simon Monaghan (leere)

'Inner Sanctuaries, City Histories' by leere and
'Seven Sisters Of Eldonian Space' by leere are available to order online at:

www.waterstones.com